Pet Projects

Designer DOG Projects

Loads of cool craft projects inside

Isabel Thomas

raintree
a Capstone company — publishers for children

Raintree is an imprint of Capstone Global Library Limited, a company incorporated in England and Wales having its registered office at 7 Pilgrim Street, London, EC4V 6LB – Registered company number: 6695582

www.raintree.co.uk
myorders@raintree.co.uk

Edited by Helen Cox Cannons and Holly Beaumont
Designed by Philippa Jenkins
Picture research by Tracy Cummins
Production by Helen McCreath
Originated by Capstone Global Library Ltd
Printed and bound in China

ISBN 978 1 406 29822 2
19 18 17 16 15
10 9 8 7 6 5 4 3 2 1

British Library Cataloguing in Publication Data
A full catalogue record for this book is available from the British Library.

Acknowledgements
We would like to thank the following for permission to reproduce photographs:
Alamy: Tetra Images, Cover Bottom Left; Shutterstock: absolutimages, 20 Bottom Left, bluecrayola, 29 Top, Brooke Whatnall, Design Element, Lightcontrol, 19 Bottom, Sue McDonald, 1, Multiple use.

All other photography by Capstone Studio: Karon Dubke.

Every effort has been made to contact copyright holders of material reproduced in this book. Any omissions will be rectified in subsequent printings if notice is given to the publisher.

All the internet addresses (URLs) given in this book were valid at the time of going to press. However, due to the dynamic nature of the internet, some addresses may have changed, or sites may have changed or ceased to exist since publication. While the author and publisher regret any inconvenience this may cause readers, no responsibility for any such changes can be accepted by either the author or the publisher.

Safety instructions for adult helper
Some of the projects in this book involve steps that should only be carried out by an adult – these are indicated in the text. Always follow the instructions carefully.

Contents

Look out for the paw-print icons. These tell you how long each project will take.

= up to 30 minutes

= up to 1 hour

= more than 1 hour

Dotty about dogs!

If you're dotty about dogs, you'll love the projects in this book. If you are lucky enough to have a pet pooch, or just love those wagging tails and adorable eyes, there is so much to make and do.

- ✪ Make gifts for dog-loving friends or relatives
- ✪ Decorate your bedroom with doggy designs
- ✪ Create homemade dog treats and playthings
- ✪ Throw a pooch party!

At the back of the book you'll find a link to a web page packed with templates to use in the projects, and tips on how to use them to create designs of your own!

Getting started

Before starting each project, read the instructions carefully and make sure you have everything you need. Find out if you will need an adult to help with any of the steps. If you are planning to reuse an object, or decorate walls, clothes or furniture, check that it's OK first.

Doggy bags
page 27

Cup cakes
page 26

Sausage dog
page 8

Working safely

Work in an area where you can make a mess, using newspaper to protect the table or floor. If you are using paint or glue, make sure you open the windows or work outside. Keep pets away while you are crafting. Never use paint or glue near a pet – the fumes can be dangerous for animals.

Pet view

Look out for my tips on dog care as you scamper through the book!

Things... to keep in your craft kit

- Scissors, pens, pencils, paints, paintbrush, ruler, sticky tape and PVA glue.

- Scraps of pretty fabric, paper, card, newspapers and magazines.

- Boxes, jars and containers with interesting shapes (wash and dry food containers before storing them).

- Pretty found objects such as feathers, stones and buttons.

- Sewing materials such as needle and thread, wool, yarn, ribbons and trimmings.

Get crafty with paper

Paper is so versatile. Let your creativity off the lead with these pooch-inspired projects.

Doggy découpage

Découpage (say day-coo-paj) is a way of decorating with cut or torn paper. It's a great way to recycle magazines or wrapping paper. Use découpage to cover anything from a notebook to a table, and transform everyday objects into a dog-lover's delight!

1. Cut or tear the paper into pieces. These should be big enough to show off the pictures or patterns.

2. Paint a small area of the notebook cover with diluted PVA glue. Stick on pieces of cut or torn paper, overlapping the edges.

3. Repeat until you have covered the notebook with pictures, and leave to dry.

4. To seal and protect your design, brush with a coat of diluted PVA glue. Leave to dry overnight before adding a second coat.

You will need:

- dog magazines, wrapping paper or pet store catalogues
- diluted PVA glue (3 parts glue to 1 part water)
- paintbrush
- new notebook with a hard cover

Smooth out trapped air bubbles.

You can use this technique to decorate mirror frames, boxes or shelves!

Pet view

Use your notebook to keep a record of my feeding habits, training and exercise routines, vaccinations and vet visits. Knowing me really well will help you spot if I get ill or injured.

5 books... every dog lover should read

Head down to your local library to track down these brilliant reads.

- *The Incredible Journey* by Sheila Burnford
- *The Hundred and One Dalmatians* by Dodie Smith
- *Because of Winn-Dixie* by Kate DiCamillo
- *A Dog So Small* by Philippa Pearce
- *Shiloh* by Phyllis Reynolds Naylor

Upcycle!

Don't throw out old clothes and containers. Recycle them into awesome accessories for you and your dog, and help save the planet at the same time.

Cute and cosy sausage dog

Sparkly, spotty or striped – old tights and socks can be used to make super-cute sausage dogs that guard your room in chilly weather!

1. Cut one leg from the pair of tights. Stuff it with old clothes, carrier bags or foam packaging to make a sausage-dog shape.

2. Loop an elastic band around the opening to hold the stuffing in place. Loop another elastic band around the toe of the tights to make your dog's nose.

3. Cut the ends from the socks, and pin or sew them on to the dog's head to make floppy ears.

4. Add a ribbon collar, and button eyes.

You will need:

- old pair of woolly tights
- old pair of socks
- scraps of fabric
- buttons
- two elastic bands
- needle and thread
- stuffing material

> The sausage dog makes a great decoration for the end of your bed. Fashion fabulous and toasty warm!

Pet view

Use a sausage-dog doorstop to keep draughts away from my sleeping spot. I may have a fantastic furry coat, but I still need a warm, dry place to snooze.

In the frame

Bottle tops and jar lids can become colourful frames for pet photos.

1 Clean and dry each lid, and cut your photo and a circle of foam to fit inside.

2 Slot your photo into place over the foam. Glue a magnetic strip on the back of the lid so it sticks to a fridge or radiator.

You will need:

- jar lids or bottle tops
- pet photo
- sheet of craft foam
- buttons
- glue
- scissors
- magnets

A collection of lid frames is a fun way to display a larger photograph.

Making a "T"-riffic tug toy

T-shirt toys in pretty colours make a great gift for fashionable dog owners.

1. Carefully cut the T-shirts or towels into at least 15 long strips, each around 5 cm (2 in.) wide. You will need to use at least two adult-sized T-shirts, or three child's T-shirts. Gently stretch each strip lengthways, so that it curls up into a tube.

2. Gather the strips and knot them together tightly at one end.

3. Pin the knot to a cushion to keep it in place for the next step. Divide the bunch of strips into three, and plait tightly.

4. When the plait is 20 to 30 cm (8 to 12 in.) long, finish with a tight knot. Trim the ends so they are as short as possible.

You will need:

- old, clean T-shirts (you could also use old towels or tea towels)
- scissors
- safety pin

> T-shirt toys are perfect for playing tug, fetch or hide-and-seek.

!

WARNING!
Don't use T-shirts with embellishments or transfers, or towels that have been used for cleaning with chemicals.

TOP TIP

Cut strips quickly by cutting straight across the bottom of a T-shirt. Snip the loop to make a longer strip.

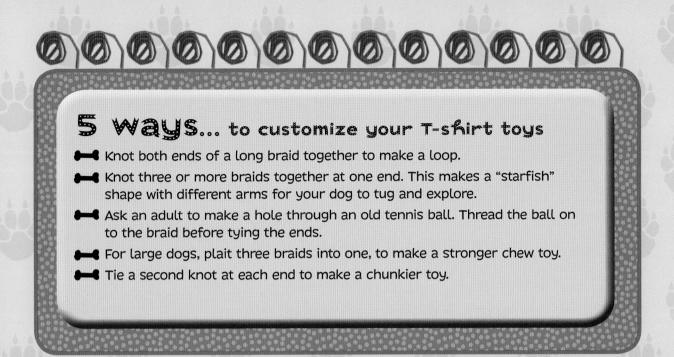

5 ways... to customize your T-shirt toys

- Knot both ends of a long braid together to make a loop.
- Knot three or more braids together at one end. This makes a "starfish" shape with different arms for your dog to tug and explore.
- Ask an adult to make a hole through an old tennis ball. Thread the ball on to the braid before tying the ends.
- For large dogs, plait three braids into one, to make a stronger chew toy.
- Tie a second knot at each end to make a chunkier toy.

Sleeping spot

If you can get your paws on loads of old T-shirts, try weaving a colourful, washable rug for your pet. Join several strips together to make longer strips, and then plait them into a tight, flat braid. Coil the braid into a spiral and stitch into place.

Pet view

Make sure you play with me every day! Always watch me carefully when I'm playing with toys. If I chew off any small pieces, throw them away.

Funky fabric projects

Raid your local fabric shop for off-cuts with pretty patterns. A touch of sewing magic transforms them into accessories for a pampered pet.

Handy hound organizer

This is the perfect place to store your dog's grooming kit and accessories. Why not make one for your bedroom too?

1 Each pocket uses one letter-sized rectangle of fabric. Simply pin on a piece of A4 paper and cut around it. Fold it in half lengthways and pin to hold in place.

2 Make a horizontal cut across the front layer only, 4 cm (1½ in.) from the top.

3 Thread your needle and sew the three open sides of the rectangle together, around 1 cm (½ in.) in from the edge of the fabric. Reach into the opening, and turn the pocket inside out to hide the seams.

You will need:

- Letter-sized pieces of different fabrics – collect off-cuts, or ask if it's ok to recycle old clothes, sheets or curtains
- scissors
- pins, needle, thread
- buttons

Use cotton to make your organizer easy to wash.

 **TOP TIP**

Ask an adult to help you use a sewing machine for a neater, stronger finish.

4 Use a ruler to mark a dot 2 cm (1 in.) diagonally from each corner of the pocket.

5 Sew a button on to each of the bottom dots. Cut and stitch a buttonhole into each of the top corners, centred on the dots.

6 Make as many pockets as you need to store your dog's items. Simply button them together to make the organizer grow as your dog does!

7 Thread short pieces of ribbon through the buttonholes to hang your pocket.

Brilliant bandana

A stylish bandana looks adorable, and keeps your dog warm in cold weather. Learn how to make one in minutes!

1 Cut a 35 to 70 cm (14 to 27 in.) square of light cotton fabric. The exact size will depend on the size of the dog you are making it for.

2 Fold the square diagonally and cut down the fold to make two triangles.

3 Put one triangle on the other, with the patterned sides facing in. Pin and then sew them together, leaving a 10 cm (4 in.) gap.

4 Reach into the gap and turn the bandana inside out. Split a small piece of Velcro and sew to either end of the longest edge. The bandana is ready to wear.

You will need:

- cotton fabric
- pins, needle, thread, scissors
- Velcro

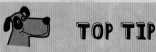

TOP TIP

To work out the size of the square you need, do this sum: (Collar measurement + 2 cm) / sq root of 2 = length of sides of square

5 projects... with fabric paint

Fabric paint can be used to customize clothes, furniture and other objects. Always ask permission first and work carefully as fabric paints are permanent!

- Paint paw prints or dog shapes on to curtains. You'll find stencil-making instructions and a link to the templates on page 31.
- Use a pin to transfer a doggy design on to craft foam. Cut the foam shape out, dip it into fabric paint, and use it to print patterns on a bag or pencil case.
- Create cuddly cushions covered with paw prints in rainbow colours.
- Add doggy designs to a T-shirt or dress.
- Paint a solid silhouette over the patterned fabric pockets on page 12.

Embroider your dog's name or your initials on to the bandana!

Pup art projects

Dogs have always inspired artists. Now it's your turn! Start with this portable paw print.

Salty dog key ring

🐾 🐾 🐾

Salt dough is a super-cheap sculpting material, safe enough for your dog to stand on.

1 Mix the flour and salt together. Slowly add the water, stirring to make a dough. Knead it with your hands for a few minutes, adding a few more drops of water if it looks like it is cracking.

2 Roll the dough out on greaseproof paper until it is around 1 cm (½ in.) thick.

3 Spread a sheet of newspaper on the floor, and put the salt dough on top. Hold out a treat for your dog, while an adult helps guide one of your dog's paws on to the salt dough for a few moments to leave a paw print.

4 Cut around the paw print using a cookie cutter or the rim of a glass.

5 To make a key ring, use a cocktail stick to carefully poke a hole through the medallion.

You will need:

- 150 g (5 oz.) flour
- 75 g (2½ oz.) salt
- 60 ml water
- greaseproof paper and newspaper
- cookie cutter or glass
- cocktail sticks
- paints and paintbrushes
- black marker pen
- key ring attachment

Pet view

Salt dough is safe for me to stand on, but don't let me eat it!

6 Leave the salt dough to dry out (this will take a day or two).

7 Paint the medallion and paw print and, when the paint has dried, use a marker pen to write your dog's name on the back. You can attach it to the key ring using a bright, contrasting thread.

Brush on a coat of watered down PVA glue or clear varnish to seal your design.

 **TOP TIP**

Speed up the drying time by asking an adult to bake the model in an oven at 165°C (329°F) for 1 hour.

Pots of puppy love

There are loads of ways to get creative with your spare salt dough. Try adding a head, paws and tail to a flower pot!

Doggy drawings

It can be hard to draw dogs - they're not very good at holding a pose!
Try this technique for drawing perfect pet portraits from photographs.

1 Use the marker pen to draw a 15 × 15-cm grid of 1-cm squares on the plastic film. Paperclip it to your favourite dog photograph.

2 Lightly draw a matching grid on your drawing paper, in pencil. If you want to make your portrait larger than the photograph, doube the length and width of each square.

3 Use the grid lines as a guide, transfer the main details from each square of the photograph to the corresponding square on the paper.

4 Remove the grid from the photograph and rub out the pencil gridlines, leaving the outline details. Use colouring pencils or pastels to complete your pet portrait.

You will need:

- sheet of clear plastic film (try a stationery shop, or look out for stiff clear plastic packaging)
- fine permanent marker pen
- ruler and rubber
- drawing paper and pencil

TOP TIP

It can be helpful to label the rows and columns with letters and numbers.

TOP TIP
If you are able to print on to clear plastic film, you'll find a grid template on the website (see page 31).

Pet projects make perfect presents.

5 tips... for taking great dog photographs

- Take pictures in your dog's favourite places. Your pet is more likely to be relaxed and in a good mood.
- If you are using a digital camera, turn off the sound and the flash. Your dog is less likely to notice the camera.
- Get down so your camera is at your dog's eye level. This might mean lying on the grass, or kneeling on the ground.
- Use treats to encourage your dog to stay in one place, or games to get her to move around.
- Perfectly posed shots are boring! Take pictures that showcase your pet's quirks, to capture their unique personality.

Kitchen creations

Every dog loves a treat, but did you know that some shop-bought pet treats have unhealthy ingredients, such as sugar, milk and colourings? Make these naturally delicious alternatives.

Fresh breath biscuits

A little dry dog food every day can keep your dog's teeth clean, meaning healthy gums and fresher breath.

1. Ask an adult to heat the oven to 190°C (375°F).

2. Chop the mint and parsley leaves.

3. Mix everything together in a large bowl to make a sticky dough.

4. Sprinkle a little flour on a flat surface, and roll out the dough to around 1 cm (½ in.) thick.

5. Use a cookie cutter to cut biscuit shapes, and put them on a greased and lined baking tray.

6. Ask an adult to cook them in the oven for 20 minutes.

7. Leave the biscuits to cool, then store them in a tin or plastic box with a lid.

You will need:

- 200 g (7 oz.) wholemeal flour
- 50 g (1¾ oz.) mint leaves
- 50 g (1¾ oz.) fresh parsley
- 50 ml vegetable oil
- 1 egg
- 100 ml water

Makes about 30 biscuits

Pet view

Bad breath can be a sign that I'm unhealthy, so always check with a vet. It's a good idea to clean my teeth too – but only with a special doggy toothpaste and toothbrushes.

Bran bites

Freshly made treats will keep your best friend in tip-top condition.

1 Ask an adult to heat the oven to 175°C (350°F).

2 Mix the flour and bran with the grated vegetables and cheese.

3 In a separate bowl, beat the milk, maple syrup and oil together using a fork.

4 Add the wet ingredients to the dry ingredients, and mix with your hands to bring the dough together.

5 Break off small balls of dough and put them on a non-stick baking sheet.

6 Gently press down on each ball to flatten it into a dog biscuit shape.

7 Ask an adult to bake the biscuits in the oven for 25 minutes.

8 When the biscuits are completely cool, store them in a tin or plastic container with a lid.

You will need:

- 300 g (10½ oz.) wholemeal flour
- 2 tablespoons bran
- 1 courgette, grated
- 1 carrot, grated
- 50 g (1¾ oz.) cheese, grated
- 30 ml vegetable oil
- 1 tablespoon maple syrup
- 200 ml milk

Give your dog one biscuit at a time as a treat.

Pet placemat

Dogs can be messy eaters, but this pet placemat makes spills easier to clean up. Download and print a template (see page 31) and transfer it on to patterned paper. Cut out and glue the shape on to a large sheet of card, then have the placemat laminated at your local print shop.

Dog-tastic DIY projects

Even if your dog isn't allowed in your bedroom, you can fill it with reminders of your BFF - best furry friend!

Doggy wall art

Combine a doggy design with a pretty pattern to make wall art that gets tails wagging. Remember to ask permission first!

1 Choose a doggy design – you'll find a link to lots of fantastic templates on page 31. Enlarge the design before you print it, or print first and use a photocopier to enlarge it on to A3 paper.

2 Cut out the enlarged shape, then draw around it on the back of patterned sticky-backed plastic, wrapping paper or wallpaper. Cut out the shape carefully.

3 Try out the shape in different places, such as walls or furniture. When you are happy with the position, peel off the backing and press it into place. If you are using wrapping paper or wallpaper, stick it down with PVA glue or wallpaper paste. Brush over a coat of watered-down PVA glue or clear varnish to stop the edges peeling away.

You will need:

- tracing paper
- scissors and brush
- sticky-backed plastic or patterned wallpaper
- PVA glue or clear varnish

 **TOP TIP**

Try mixing patterns or silhouettes for a custom look.

Muddy pawprints

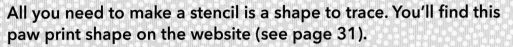

All you need to make a stencil is a shape to trace. You'll find this paw print shape on the website (see page 31).

1. Transfer the paw-print design on to card, using the tips on page 31. Leave a large border.

2. Cut away the inside of the shape, using small scissors, or ask an adult to help you cut it out using a craft knife.

3. Position the stencil on the wall, using masking tape to hold it in place.

4. Dip an old toothbrush in acrylic paint and rub your finger along the toothbrush to spatter the paint on to the wall. Carefully remove the stencil from the wall.

5. When the stencil is dry, reposition it on the wall and add another paw print. Repeat to create a trail of "muddy" prints.

You will need:

- tracing paper
- cardboard
- masking tape
- scissors
- paint
- old toothbrush or sponge

TOP TIP

You can create a similar effect using a sponge.

Customize the design using colours that match other objects in your bedroom, such as the curtains or bedspread.

Pom-pom mania

Cute, fluffy and versatile, pom-poms can be used to decorate everything from presents to pet baskets! Learn the basic technique first, and then let your imagination run wild.

1 Print the pom-pom template (see page 31) and transfer it on to thick cardboard. Cut out two identical discs.

2 Place one disc on top of the other. Wind wool around the discs, working your way around until they are covered in a thick layer of wool. If you run out of wool, just knot a new piece on and keep going. The more layers of wool, the thicker and fluffier your pom-pom will be.

3 Carefully cut through the wool at the edge of the discs, a little at a time.

You will need:

- colourful wool
- thick cardboard
- scissors

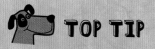 TOP TIP

Enlarge the template to make pom-poms in different sizes. The bigger the pom-pom, the more wool you will need.

4 Take a long piece of wool and carefully slide it between the discs, tying a knot at the bottom. Tighten the knot to tie all the strands together.

5 Slide the cardboard discs out, and fluff up the pom-pom.

 **TOP TIP**

Leave the ends of the knotted piece of wool hanging out of the pom-pom, to help attach it to other things.

5 things... to make with pom-poms

🦴 If you have lots of wool (and time!) make a hundred pom-poms. Thread them on to a square of strong fabric, working from the centre out, to make a rug your dog will love to curl up on.

🦴 Tie pom-poms together and trim them into shape, to make cute fluffy puppies. Glue on felt ears and a nose.

🦴 Download a poodle template (see page 31) and transfer it on to card. Glue on pom-poms to make a fluffy wall hanging.

🦴 Embroider a puppy face on to a plain woollen hat. Sew on pom-pom ears to turn it into a fashion must-have.

🦴 Thread colourful pom-poms on to embroidery silk or yarn to make strings of pom-pom bunting.

Throw a pooch party!

Your dog is part of the family, so make him or her part of holidays and celebrations, too.

Say it with flour

Dog lovers will go crazy for these cute cupcakes.

1 Cover each cupcake in buttercream icing.

2 Use a small biscuit to build up the shape of the muzzle, then cover it with another layer of icing.

3 Spoon some of the buttercream into a piping bag and gently squeeze it out to form the ears.

4 Add a nose and eyes using the black writing icing.

5 Using the pink writing icing, add a small tongue to finish off your panting pooch.

You will need:

- 12 undecorated cupcakes
- buttercream icing in different colours
- small biscuits
- piping kit
- writing icing in black and pink

Make the ears smaller or larger depending on the type of dog you are trying to create.

5 ideas... for gifts and favours

These projects make great gifts for dog owners, and double up as party favours!

- Collect clean, empty jars. In neat layers, add the dry ingredients for making the cute cupcakes on page 26 and tie on the instructions for making the recipe at home.

- Make the doggy bandana on page 14, embroidered with the dog's name or owner's initials.

- Make a pretty T-shirt toy in the dog owner's favourite colours (see page 10).

- Make a cute pom-pom puppy for every guest – or teach them how to make their own for crafty party fun.

- Decorate paper bags with doggy faces and paper ears, and fill them with dry doggy treats.

Pet view

Did you know that some human treats, such as chocolate and raisins, can be poisonous for dogs? Only offer me specially made doggy treats, and never leave chocolate where I can find it.

Pet piñata

A piñata is an exciting party prop that is broken open to reveal the treats inside. This dog-safe version is a fun way to make your pooch part of the party.

1 Blow up the balloon and hang it over a waterproof surface. Tear the newspaper into strips.

2 Whisk the flour and 250 ml of water in a pan to make a paste. Whisk in the rest of the water. Ask an adult to bring the mixture to the boil for you, stirring all the time, then take it off the heat and leave it to cool completely.

3 Dip a strip of newspaper into the cold paste and lay it on the balloon. Repeat this until the whole balloon is covered with strips.

4 Leave the balloon to dry overnight. Pop the balloon, and pull it out of the paper shell. Make sure no pieces of balloon are left inside.

5 Carefully cut more holes in the piñata – the more holes there are, the easier the game will be.

6 Put some dog treats in the piñata and give it to your pet. Roll it, chase it, squash it, shake it… they'll have fun trying to get the treats out!

You will need:

- balloon
- newspaper
- string
- 150 g (5 oz.) plain flour
- 500 ml water
- pan and whisk
- paintbrush
- scissors
- dry dog treats

Make the holes bigger than your treats.

Learn a party trick

Learn to "dance" with your dog by teaching them how to leg weave.

- Take a healthy treat in each hand and stand feet apart.

- Guide your dog through your legs from front to back and around your right leg to the front, using the treat in your right hand.

- Give them the treat to say "Well done!", then use the treat in your left hand to guide them through your legs again and back around your left leg.

- When your clever dog has completed a full figure of eight, reward them with a treat.

Like all tricks, your dog will learn best if you practise little and often. Use the word "weave" every time, and give your dog plenty of praise. Eventually they'll learn to do a figure of eight when they hear the word "weave", without the need for hand signals.

Pet view

Balloons scare me when they pop, and could harm me if I swallow them. Always keep balloons away from your dog. Piñatas for people are often made using glue. Never give your dog a "people" piñata.

Dog facts

5 facts... for dog lovers

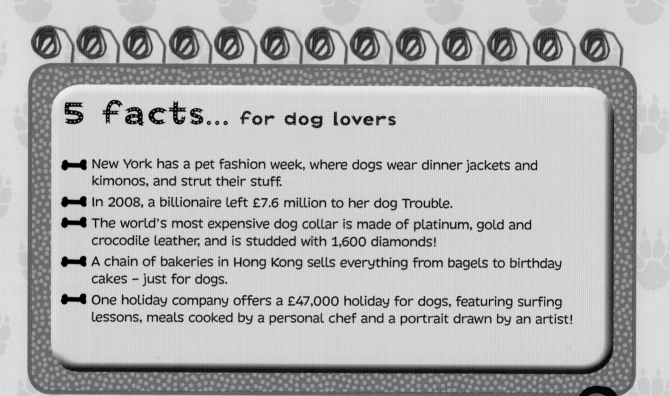

- New York has a pet fashion week, where dogs wear dinner jackets and kimonos, and strut their stuff.
- In 2008, a billionaire left £7.6 million to her dog Trouble.
- The world's most expensive dog collar is made of platinum, gold and crocodile leather, and is studded with 1,600 diamonds!
- A chain of bakeries in Hong Kong sells everything from bagels to birthday cakes – just for dogs.
- One holiday company offers a £47,000 holiday for dogs, featuring surfing lessons, meals cooked by a personal chef and a portrait drawn by an artist!

Find out more

The Young Kennel Club has lots of information for young dog fans.
www.ykc.org.uk

Battersea Cats & Dogs Home has a website with educational resources and lots of things to make and do.
www.battersea.org.uk

Visit the RSPCA for tips on caring for pet dogs.
www.rspca.org.uk/adviceandwelfare/pets/dogs

Crufts is the world's largest dog show, and a great place to spot your favourite breeds.
www.crufts.org.uk

Templates

Visit **www.raintree.co.uk/content/download** and select "Designer Dog Projects" to download free templates to use with the projects in this book. You can also use them to create your own doggy designs. Once you have printed a template, follow these tips to transfer it to the material you are working with.

• Use masking tape to hold a sheet of tracing or baking paper over your chosen design and draw over the outline with a soft pencil.

• Tape the paper on to the surface you'd like to transfer the picture to.

• Draw over the lines using a pen with a hard point.

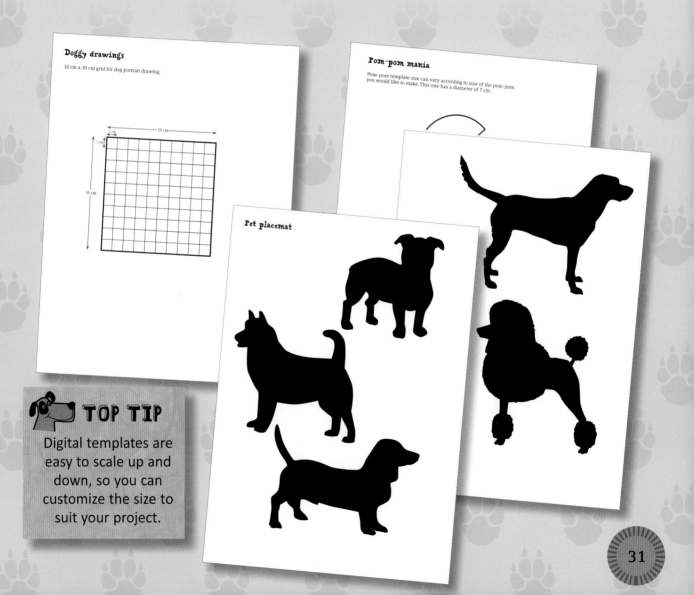

Doggy drawings

10 cm x 10 cm grid for dog portrait drawing.

Pom-pom mania

Pom-pom template size can vary according to size of the pom-pom you would like to make. This one has a diameter of 7 cm.

Pet placemat

TOP TIP

Digital templates are easy to scale up and down, so you can customize the size to suit your project.

Index